Contents

Introduction

Ever since primitive man found the urge to decorate his cave, the legacy of his efforts, thousands of years ago, has passed on to his descendants. Today, countless numbers of people, in every walk of life, satisfy this same urge of self expression by stamping their individuality on their homes and dwellings.

But it was only thirty or so years ago, following the privations of the war and the release of special materials that were developed during it, that the do-it-yourself movement really began to make great strides. Now it has become a multi-million-pound industry and a way of life for many householders who have found pleasure and profit in maintaining their homes to the highest possible standard, increasing the value as every year passes.

With the continuing public demand for materials, manufacturers have responded with new products designed to make the work easier and more satisfying which enable anyone with a little patience to equal the best and most costly work of the tradesman. When you consider that by supplying your own labour you are reducing the costs of home decorating by at least 75 per cent you will see it makes sense to do it yourself.

In the following pages you will note that we have come a long way since the Victorian music hall audiences sang 'Father painted the parlour and you couldn't see Pa for paint', and you will, I hope, be encouraged to make interior decorating a part of your leisure which will be both rewarding and pleasurable.

Note Measurements in the book are given in metric and their imperial equivalents, except for paintbrushes, which are sold in imperial sizes only.

Practical Considerations

With such a bewildering variety of decorating products available, it is not easy for the beginner to decide which will best suit his particular purpose. While the merits and uses of most products are explained in subsequent chapters it cannot be stressed enough that the basic factors of high-class work are to choose the right materials and to ensure that all surfaces are adequately prepared to receive them.

It is important also to consider cost. There are so many bargain offers available that you can be misled into thinking, for example, that half-price unbranded emulsion paint will do as well as an established brand made by a reputable manufacturer. I am not decrying special cut-price offers made possible by bulk-buying and competition, but it is wise to remember that it always pays to buy the best you can afford.

With so many formulations in paint, where the ingredients vary

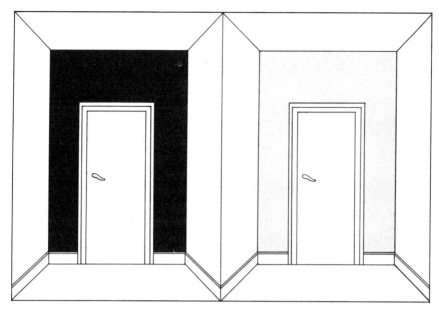

Different effects can be created by using
darker or lighter colours ; dark colours
'advance', light colours 'recede'

considerably, it is also good advice to
keep to the products of one company
where research has shown that its top
coat of gloss paint 'marries' perfectly
with its undercoat.

There are several reasons for
decorating : it may be that everything
looks shabby and you want to achieve
an entirely different effect from the
original. Here colour and textures,
explained later, will have to be
considered, without going to the
expense of changing curtains and soft
furnishings. Of course, if you are
changing these as well you have much
greater scope.

Most people can picture colour,
pattern and texture in a room (women
have a particular ability for it), but if
you are short of ideas look at the various
schemes detailed in the literature
available in the decorators' shops.
There are plenty of leaflets available,
while sound advice is generally
available in the specialist shops.

Once you have a clear picture in
your mind it is essential to put it down
on paper, but refer to pages 6–7 first,
where certain fundamentals are set out
in order to produce an overall effect
which is going to please. It is asking for
failure if you rush out and buy paint
and wall-coverings before you know
exactly what your requirements are.

Colour in the Home

When you look at a rainbow you are seeing the effect produced when natural light is split up by the refraction of millions of raindrops into its constituent parts—red, orange, yellow, green, blue, indigo and violet.

This spectrum is the basis of the colour consultant's colour 'wheel' and the cards which can be obtained in most decorating outlets. They will tell you that colours at the red end are 'advancing, warm colours' while those at the violet end are 'receding and cool', and that certain basic rules of using colour in the home should be followed.

But as colour is a matter of individual preference it is wise to work out colour schemes which will stamp your individuality on them; schemes which will take into account the aspect of your rooms, their sizes, the lighting, the positions of windows and doors, the furniture, soft furnishings and floorings.

In spite of this there are still some basic rules to remember as the choice of colour can make or mar a room. Warm colours will make a north-facing room more cheerful, while the use of the cooler ones in sunny rooms promotes a lightness which can be refreshing. Small rooms should always be decorated with light materials as, generally speaking, they create a feeling of spaciousness.

These few pointers may help. The primary colours are red, yellow and blue. Red is the boldest, warmest, most exciting colour. Set it off with white. Orange goes well with cream, or contrasted with a shade of turquoise.

Yellow is cheerful and sunny, ideal for cold rooms. It tones well with tan and contrasts with greens and blues. Blue is cool and cold and tones with its own shades, but contrasts with the lighter greens.

For the rest there are the neutral colours of white, grey and black which play a most important part in any colour scheme. Greens, browns and purples in their various shades also have an important part to play.

Apart from colour, texture should always be considered and perhaps incorporated in the décor.

The use of the correct colour combination can produce significant effects on the apparent size of a room.

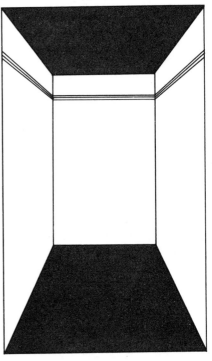

A ceiling that is too high can be 'brought down' by using a bright warm

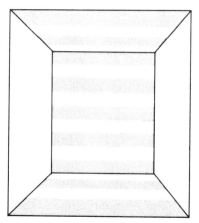

colour or a dark rich one. A low ceiling can be 'raised' by using a light colour and a wall-covering which has a

clearly defined vertical stripe pattern. Similarly a narrow corridor or hall can be made to look wider by the

use of a bold horizontal design. The illustrations show how these effects can be produced.

As in most things a balanced design must be the result of careful planning. Here your decorating shop can be of the greatest help. When you have to take into account your carpets and curtains, etc, try to take a small colour sample of them with you.

At the shop, collect the various colour cards and, where available, samples of wall-coverings. Look at them carefully in both natural and artificial light as the colours can vary considerably.

Remember that fashions change. One year the 'in' colour is avocado, the next a rich shade of purple. Today, browns are coming back into fashion. Unfortunately many paint manufacturers have departed from the practice of calling a paint by its shade. Instead we ask for paint with a name recognized only by students of art history and only by seeing a colour card can we connect the two !

Have confidence in your judgment. If you want to be a little daring don't let anyone put you off. Some original bold ideas have worked out extremely well.

Finally, if you are starting from the very beginning and moving into a first home, there are booklets available which set out very clearly how wall-coverings, fabric and paints are branded together. The producers supply the three basic items under one brand name which makes your choice extremely simple.

Preparing to Decorate

You can give a face-lift to a small room with nothing more than two or three cans of paint, a couple of brushes (or one brush and a roller) and a pair of steps ; but this would merely produce a cover-up job which might only last for a few months, giving you a much more difficult and lengthy task to undertake at a later date. So, however small or simple the job is, it is worthwhile doing it properly.

Equipment

To achieve good results it is important to do the necessary preparation, and there are several basic items of equipment available that will help to make this task easier.

To start with you will need : a bucket of hot water and a sponge to remove dirt and grease ; a stripping knife or scraper 7.5–9cm (3–3½in) wide, for removing ordinary wallpaper ; a shaving hook for removing paint and dirt from angles in window frames and door mouldings ; a pack of various grades of glasspaper to rub down walls after paper removal and for 'keying' a previously painted surface ; a wire brush if you are removing wallpaper that has been painted ; a paint stripper (see pages 14–15) to remove loose paint ; a dusting brush or tack rags (these are re-usable pads impregnated with a non-sticky adhesive) to remove dust from surfaces to be painted.

For applying paint it is best to use paintbrushes of different widths : a 1in brush for working in corners, a 2in brush for larger areas, and a 4in brush or roller for emulsion paint. A small paint kettle 12.5cm (5in) into which the paint can be strained is useful, as large cans are awkward and heavy to carry.

Paint brushes must be looked after ; those used for traditional gloss and oil-based paints will need cleaning in white spirit or turpentine, unless otherwise stated by the manufacturer.

Preparation of Surfaces

If you have windows to paint, and you think it will be difficult to keep the painted edges straight, you can use masking tape on the glass so that the applied paint will slightly overlap the frame *and* the glass ; or you can use a small aluminium paint shield called 'George' but if you use this appliance wipe the back edge of it each time you move it along. Practise with it before you start painting.

Experience has shown that merely to rub down defective painted surfaces, for example those that are blistered and flaking, is not sufficient ; neither is it good practice to add coat after coat of paint where the additional thickness makes doors and windows difficult to open and close. In these cases removal of the paint is vital and this can be done mechanically, chemically or by means of heat.

Paint can be effectively scraped off a flat surface with the double-bladed action of a Skarsten scraper (see illustration) which has a serrated blade to cut through the paint film and a razor-sharp edge for finishing.

Power-operated sanding machines can be used for paint removal but their use is rather limited, except on large flat areas. An abrasive disc on a rubber pad fitted as an attachment to an electric drill must be used with care otherwise it can easily make deep score lines in the woodwork or plaster. Chemical methods include the use of paint strippers of several types, but in inexperienced hands these are inclined to be a bit messy.

Now that the old type of petrol and paraffin blowlamps have been superseded by very efficient gas blowtorches, thick coats of paint can be removed quite easily. The correct method of doing this is shown on page 15.

In removing stubborn wallpaper, you may find that you have dug into the plaster beneath ; any such imperfections in a wall that is to be papered or painted should be rubbed down or filled. A springy filling knife should be used for this—never use a stripping knife.

In addition to walls and woodwork, the ceiling will also need preparation. To wash off the ceiling and paint it you will need a stout pair of steps, a strong plank or scaffold board and a box or firm chair on which to rest one end of the board. If you use a chair, tie the board to it to prevent it from slipping off.

Ceiling work can be very tiring if you are not accustomed to it. To alleviate this you should get as close as you can to the surface on which you are working. (See Ceilings on page 34.)

Once these first attempts at decorating have proved successful, you will be encouraged to tackle more ambitious projects around the home, for which you will need other items of equipment. These are dealt with in later sections.

Plastic bucket and sponge

Stripping knife

Scraper hook

Skarsten scraper

Glass paper

Wire brush

Dusting brush

Step-ladder

Paints

Brush cleaner

Ready-mixed filler

Paint tray and roller

Paint kettle

Brushes

'George' paint shield

Masking tape

9

Choice of Materials

Twenty-five years ago almost the only materials available to the amateur decorator were various types of distemper, ceiling-white and oil-paints. For the walls the only non-exotic material was the standard wallpaper made from pulp, and these products were only available through trade sources. What a difference there is today when every product used in the construction and decoration of a property is available to everyone !

Consider the liquid products for ceiling decoration. There are gloss and semi-gloss paints, some with non-drip properties, matt, silk and eggshell finishes, textured and embossed expanded polystyrene tiles with insulating and acoustic properties, fibrous plaster motifs, mirror tiles, wood panelling, extruded aluminium channelling to support insulation, or coloured plastic panels behind which is concealed lighting. And, if your pocket can stand it, you can buy moulded polyurethane made to look like age-old beams with simulated woodworm and nail holes.

For redecorating or refurbishing floors there is also a bewildering choice : superb, non-slip ceramic tiles, textured linoleum, self-adhesive plastic tiles, stripwood, parquet, hardboard, plywood and tongued and grooved particle board.

When it is a case of giving a new look to walls think of these possibilities. Apart from the thinner normal wallpapers and lining papers, there are 'duplex' papers (two layers), ingrains, in which wood chips and other materials are added to give texture, flock papers made to imitate velvet, 'washable' wallpapers which are coated with a clear resin emulsion and which can be lightly sponged with soapy water, vinyl wallpapers made from a layer of PVC fused to a strong paper backing in non-pasted and ready-pasted forms, relief papers moulded to give pebble and high relief effect, and fabrics of many kinds,

the most popular being hessian. The list would not be complete without several types of cork panels and tiles, ceramic tiles, wallboards in timber and melamine coated boards, brick tiles, textured paints and a comparatively new product called 'Wonderbrix' which is spread on to a wall to give an automatic brick or stone pattern.

Quantities and Measurements

One problem which faces the amateur decorator is how to adjust his requirements to metrication. While it is true that, for the moment, both metric and imperial measures are clearly marked on most products, he should make every effort to think only in metric terms. The boxwood yardstick, so useful in marking lengths of material, should be discarded for the metre length one.

Since 1963 standard rolls of wallpaper have been in nominal lengths of 10.05m (approximately 33ft) and in normal widths 530mm (approximately 21in). But some papers are carefully marked with their own individual sizes which may vary slightly from the standard. One ready-pasted paper has these details. Dimensions: 20½in (52.1cm) wide × 33ft (10.06m) long: 56.4sq ft (5.24sq m). The slight variations are no cause for concern.

Paint is now sold in metric quantities in a standard range of tin sizes agreed by the industry—5l, 2.5l, 1l, 500ml and 250ml. Some manufacturers also supply paint in larger and smaller sizes than this standard range and not all manufacturers make, nor all shops

stock, the full range of standard sizes. However, metric marked tins must, by law, also show the quantity in imperial measure.

The thickness of glass is now defined in millimetres—no longer by weight. 18oz per sq ft is now 2mm, 24oz—3mm, 32oz—4mm and ¼in plate—6mm. Lengths and widths are specified in millimetres.

Expanded polystyrene and other ceiling tiles are sold in metric sizes, so are carpet and PVC floor tiles and PVC flooring. Mosaics are available in 300mm (1ft) squares and ceramic wall and floor tiles are also produced in metric sizes.

Metric sizes also apply to building blocks, electric cables, bolts and screws, pipe fittings and timber.

A useful guide to all materials for the handyman is available free of charge upon application to the Metrication Board, 22 Kingsway, London WC28 6LE.

Quantities of wallpaper or paint required can be worked out as follows: An average room of 3.70 × 3m (12 × 10ft) with a ceiling height of 2.50m (8ft) has these areas: ceiling approx 11m² (120sq ft), walls (excluding door and window) approx 28m² (300sq ft). If the surfaces are non-porous the ceiling would require 1l (1¾pt) of emulsion paint for each coat, while the walls would need at least 2.5 l (0.55gal).

If the walls are papered, using the standard roll, 11m × 530mm (35ft 6in × 21in), you would need approximately seven rolls of wallpaper —more if there is a distinct pattern with a large drop in the pattern.

Preparing a Room for Decorating

The complete redecoration of a room makes a number of demands upon a person who has never decorated before. It is as well to make sure the conditions are right before attempting the work.

Firstly, the room cannot be used for its normal functions for perhaps two to three days. Should it be the sitting-room or lounge/dining-room then obviously you don't want visitors, nor young children running about.

It is important, once painting has started, to ensure that the atmosphere is warm, free from dust and that the room is well ventilated without causing arctic conditions. Good lighting is vital. Before you start work you should also be in the right mood, keen to do the work and in the right physical condition. If you look upon it as a tiresome chore, tiredness becomes an easy 'get out'; good results are never obtained that way.

Of course, as explained in other chapters, you will have provided yourself with all the materials and equipment you need. Nothing is more frustrating than to find you've run out of paint (particularly if it is a colour mix) or that you are a roll of wallpaper short. The latter can be quite disastrous, as it may prove impossible to get another roll of the right shade from the same numbered batch. Even the slightest variation will be most apparent.

Once you are happy with these points the next step is to see exactly what has to be done, even before you start removing all the small items.

Make sure you have enough paint before you begin !

Curtains must be taken down, and if the room is overlooked you may want to whiten the glass to provide a measure of privacy. A lime wash would do, but a better job can be done with a product such as 'white summer cloud', which is used to reduce the sunlight on greenhouse glass.

Look for any necessary repair work. It may be in the form of rotting or rusty window frames, loose plaster or damp patches. Doors may be tight and need easing or some built-in furniture may need fitting. All constructional and repair work must be done before decorating starts.

The next step is to move out all the

small items which will impede free movement. Move all bulky items to the centre of the room and if possible cover them with a sheet of polythene. This is preferable to a dust sheet as you can easily find anything you may want.

When you have done this you will probably spot certain places where further dust-producing work is necessary. It may be rough plaster which needs rubbing down or a defective skirting board.

Get some paper and a pencil and jot these items down :

1 Ceiling and walls to be repainted. (To wash off any stains and dirt sugar soap or Flash is required.)
2 Ceiling to be lined with paper. (Estimate quantity required, paste and equipment.)
3 Walls to be painted or papered. (Estimate quantities required. Check equipment.)
4 All woodwork, doors, window frames to be prepared and repainted. (Glasspaper, tack rag, estimate quantities of paint and undercoat. Check equipment.)

Consider also the all-important task of protecting the floor while decorating. It is almost impossible to remove completely any kind of paint dropped on parquet flooring, tiled floors or fitted carpets. An overall covering of polythene fixed to all corners of the room is ideal, but could lead to a slippery surface when stripping the walls. A large dustsheet is better but they are expensive. You can get away with sheets of newspaper placed over the polythene and secured. Time spent on this preparation is worthwhile as

Newspaper can be used to protect the floor

fitted carpets, especially those fixed to solid floors, cannot be easily removed and replaced without the right equipment.

Try to arrange your work programme so that you have three to four hours without a break as you will find a great deal can be done without interruption. If you have to work in the evenings prepare a snack meal beforehand which will be very welcome when you finish for the day.

Stripping Paint

Fortunate indeed is the amateur decorator who takes over a dwelling in either its new state or one which has been well maintained by the previous occupant. In a new property a start from scratch will show the obvious imperfections and these can be remedied before any finishing work is attempted.

In other situations many problems will have to be faced. Ceilings may show cracks, and underneath the papered walls which have been emulsion painted, the plaster may be bad.

Paint on woodwork may show serious flaking or blisters and the woodwork itself may be rotten. If you suspect this, get a bradawl or sharply pointed tool and push it gently into the paintwork. If it goes in easily you will know that there is rot present. This will have to be cut out and the timber made good.

It is not always necessary to strip paintwork entirely in order to produce a suitable surface. Paint that is in fairly good condition should be washed thoroughly with Polywash, sugar soap or Flash and rinsed with cold water and dried. Only really defective paint needs to be removed either by heat, solvents or mechanical means.

Modern paint-strippers are most effective, especially the jelly types which stay in position once they are applied. They are particularly suitable on narrow mouldings and window frames where other methods could cause damage to the glass. Care should always be taken with chemical solvents and the instructions on the container must be followed carefully.

Mechanical methods of paint removal with scrapers, sanding blocks and discs on power-operated tools are also effective but often time-consuming and cannot reach internal corners where paint often accumulates. A combination of solvent and elbow grease would, of course, suffice.

Perhaps the simplest method of paint removal, once you appreciate the possible hazards, is by means of a blowtorch. The modern appliances, if used with care, are infinitely more reliable than the old type of blowtorch. In many cases the flame can be so adjusted to give a wide spread or a pencil-point width and, used in conjunction with a shavehook or stripping knife, will leave a surface ready for painting quickly and cleanly.

When using a blowtorch it is essential to bear the following points in mind. Keep the flame moving to soften and blister the paint without setting it alight, or scorching the woodwork. The flame should be applied above the stripping tool and the softened paint removed immediately and not left to harden again. Keep a bucket of water handy and drop the softened paint into it; don't let it fall on the floor unless the floor is protected with a sheet of hardboard or something similar. Paper is *not* suitable. Work on the difficult areas first, such as mouldings, using the shavehook. The surfaces must then be lightly glasspapered and any dust removed.

Using a chemical paint-stripper : the paint must be allowed to bubble before attempting to remove it

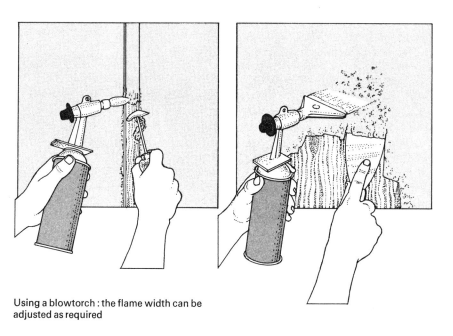

Using a blowtorch : the flame width can be adjusted as required

Paint—Types and Uses

There is such a wide variety of paint available that it is easy for the beginner to make the wrong choice by overlooking the purpose for which it is to be used.

One uses paint for three main purposes: to protect the base to which it is applied, to provide an attractive surface, perhaps coloured, to match the décor of the home, and to produce a finish which may be easily cleaned and maintained.

Most paints have the same basic ingredients of a pigment, binder and thinner. Some of the pigments are based upon metals to prevent corrosion, others are obtained from coloured earths and modern dyes. The binder, often called the 'vehicle' as it carries the pigment, is a 'sticky' material which binds the particles together, while the action of the thinner is obvious, bringing the paint to the correct consistency for ease of working and maximum coverage power.

It is always imperative to follow the manufacturers' instructions regarding the thinner to be used. It may be water in one case and turps or white spirit in another. The old rule of thumb that gloss paints should always be thinned with sub-turps no longer applies.

Even the complete beginner will be aware that today there is a considerable overlap in the suggested uses of oil-based and emulsion paints, so it will be helpful if their respective merits and uses are clearly explained.

Many oils—particularly the vegetable ones—have the capacity when drying out and exposed to the air to form a tough skin; when these drying oils are mixed with the correct resin, a free-flowing liquid paint is the result. All kinds of resins are now used. Alkyd resin produced by ICI Ltd for Dulux Gloss Finish was the first of its kind, to be followed later by polyurethane and others.

Generally, all oil-based paints have similar features—a typical painty smell in use and for some time after until they have dried out; they take several hours to dry before a second coat can be applied; they are normally thinned by white spirit or turps. They are available in many forms as sealers and primers for new or unpainted surfaces, undercoats for gloss finishes and in several types of finish such as slight sheen, eggshell, matt and very high gloss.

In choosing between the two basic types, oil paint and emulsion, convenience of use can be a deciding factor. If your time is limited and you want the minimum of upheaval in the home, emulsion paints can well satisfy your needs for it is quite feasible that you can give two coats to the ceiling, walls and woodwork of an average room in less than a day. But it would be a longer lasting job if you could split the work up and paint the woodwork with an oil-based paint two days earlier.

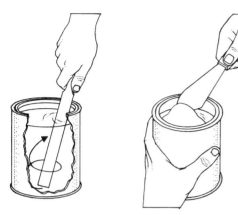
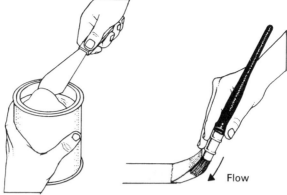 ▲ Flow

Stir liquid paint
with a spiral motion

If a skin has formed
on gloss paint, lift
it off with a knife

Using gloss paint

A Guide to Covering Capacities

	Sq Metres per Litre		Sq Yards per Litre	
	Smooth Surface	Rough Surface	Smooth Surface	Rough Surface
Liquid gloss paint	15–16		18–19	
Thyxotropic or gel gloss paint	12–14		13–17	
Undercoats	18		22	
Liquid emulsion paint	15	4	18	5
Gel type emulsion paint	11	4	13	5
Multi-purpose primer	15	4	18	5
Stabilizing primer	6	9	7	11
Alkali resisting primer	13	4	15	5
Aluminium wood primer	15		18	
Calcium plumbate	15	11	18	13
Wood primer	15	9	18	11
Zinc chromate	16	11	19	13

Paint—Types and Uses

The great merit of emulsion paint is that it has no expensive oil in its composition and its thinner is water. However, its base is often a costly synthetic resin which forms a tough film when the water has evaporated. Various resins are used, the common ones being vinyl (polyvinyl chloride and acetate, PVC and PVA) and acrylics, both of which are used widely in many other modern products. Features, common to most emulsion paints, are that they dry very quickly so that further coats can be applied ; they have hardly any smell during application or drying ; they are thinned with water and generally can be applied to most surfaces. On very porous surfaces it is advisable to apply a thinned coat of the paint to act as a primer. Various types of emulsion paints can be used as primers for wood and undercoats.

The other great merit of emulsion paint is the ease with which the equipment—paint tray, brushes, rollers, etc—can be cleaned with water. It is a bit of a chore when you have to clean appliances of oil-based paints, and many are spoiled through neglect in this respect. But there are a few quality oil-based paints which are an exception and brushes and rollers can be cleaned with water and detergent.

After this explanation of the merits of the two types of paint you may come to the conclusion that emulsion paints are the answer to all your painting requirements. However, there are two other factors to take into account—durability and appearance. Where a surface has to stand up to wear and tear, where it is subject to condensation in kitchens and bathrooms the tough paint film provided by oil-based paints is better.

As oil-based coatings are usually thicker than those of emulsion paints their quality of finish is usually preferred, and brush marks are not so apparent, particularly on woodwork. However, on walls and ceilings which have imperfect surfaces the finish obtained using emulsion paints is more satisfying.

One other aspect of paints should not be overlooked. In almost all types of paint you have the choice of liquid or non-drip paint. 'Non-drip', 'thixotropic', or 'jelly', are all terms used to describe paint which looks solid when you open the tin. The 'gel' quality is produced by an additive which is modified when you shake or stir the paint.

Non-drip paints—especially gloss—have a special appeal to beginners who not only find it difficult to apply liquid gloss paints evenly but who, until they become more proficient, get runs, sags and drips. With non-drip gloss a much thicker coating of paint can be applied and if this is brushed carefully (see following pages) splashes and drips can be avoided as the paint starts to thicken again once it is applied.

A complete range of paints for interior decoration contains the following : an aluminium primer for resinous and creosoted woods (this forms a 'leaf' over open-grained woods), metal primer, a primer/sealer for plaster and porous surfaces, undercoats, standard gloss finishes, non-drip gloss, vinyl gloss, eggshell finish, vinyl matt and vinyl silk emulsion. With such a choice there is quite clearly a paint for every purpose.

Apart from the normal paints listed above there are many others for special purposes. Bare wood containing knots, for example, should be treated with Knotting, a shellac varnish product which prevents the resin exuding from the knot. This must be applied before a primer is used.

There is also the well-known textured paint for ceilings called Artex which is applied direct to ceilings in a fairly thick consistency and then worked with a stipple brush or pad into a patterned finish. Another textured paint which has had a great appeal for amateur decorators is Polytex, made by Polycell Ltd. Designed as a self-texturing treatment for cracked ceilings and walls, it fills and covers small cracks up to 2mm ($\frac{1}{16}$in) wide and is flexible enough to keep the cracks covered even when movement occurs. It is applied by brush or roller and is available in a range of colours as well as white.

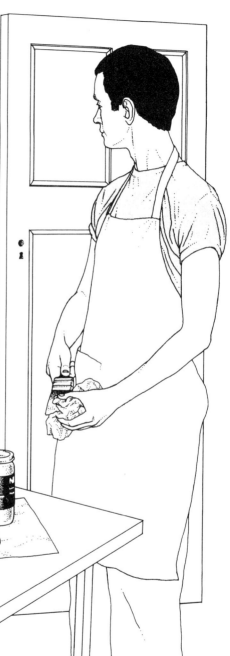

How to Paint

While the new generation of materials has made interior decorating almost foolproof it is still true that a better job can be done by following established techniques.

Take the simple matter of holding a paint brush. If you merely grasp it by the handle you restrict the movement of the wrist and you cannot get the brush to make even strokes in both directions. An experienced decorator holds the brush so that the handle lies between thumb and forefinger (as you would normally hold a pen) with the thumb on one side and the fingers on the other side of the metal ferrule (see illustration). This allows complete freedom of action and ensures that the paint flows from the thicker part of the brush towards the thinner tip.

Using a brush in this way means that you are nearer your work, which will give a much better result than if you are painting at full stretch. This applies particularly to brushes over 25mm (1in) in width, or where you want to get a free flow of gloss paint

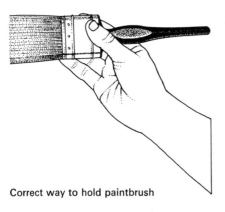

Correct way to hold paintbrush

on parts of a window frame or the panels of a door.

When using a roller you will find it more controllable (and not nearly so tiring) if, instead of locking the thumb around the fingers, you let the extended thumb lie along the handle.

One sentence contains all the advice necessary for good painting. It is 'brush on, brush out, lay off'. Each brushful of paint should be applied firmly in vertical strips without overlapping them. Follow this with horizontal strokes and then with lighter strokes, brush out vertically and horizontally. Finally, lay off with light brush strokes upward to prevent very liquid paint from producing runs and sags.

This advice applies particularly to the use of oil-based paints. With most emulsion paints, particularly the thicker non-drip variety, brushing out and laying-off may not be necessary. When using non-drip gloss paints on narrow widths of woodwork, such as window frames, it is most important not to drag the paint beyond its coverage capacity. Non-drip gloss paints, by their very nature, give thicker coatings and once applied need only light finishing off with the tip of the brush to produce a fine gloss finish.

It is not always convenient to use paint directly from the tin, especially when painting a ceiling. Use a plastic bucket for liquid paint so that you can tap the brush on its sides to remove excess paint and prevent any from running down the brush on to your hands and arms. Of course if you are using a non-drip emulsion this doesn't arise.

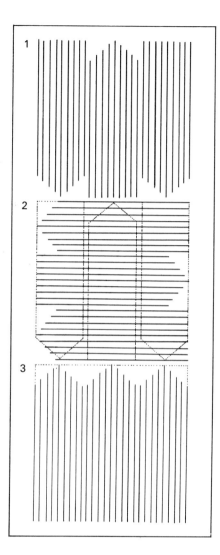

1 Brush on: up and down, then side to side
2 Brush out: repeat using light brush strokes
3 Lay off: upward light brush strokes

When you use a roller and paint tray with non-drip paint stir the paint until it is liquid and pour this into the tray, where it will start to gel again. But keep the paint moving with the roller or else you will find that the paint tends to flick off the roller in lumps.

Before walls are coated with emulsion paint you must ensure that the surface is as clean as possible and certainly has no greasy patches. Any slight rough patches on the plaster— for example, that have been left after removing wallpaper—should be rubbed down with fine-grade glasspaper and wiped off with a damp cloth.

You should start to paint at the top of the wall, after using a small brush in the corners, and paint in strips about four roller-widths wide. Work straight down to the skirting board and run the roller criss-cross over the strips. Try not to get too much overlap on the separate strips, particularly if you are using a light pastel shade of paint, otherwise these overlaps will show.

If you take a break during wall painting try to finish at a corner of the room and, if the break is likely to be for longer than an hour, pour the paint back into the can, wash the paint tray out in cold water and wrap the roller in either a damp cloth or a plastic bag. Some emulsion paints harden very quickly and you can easily ruin a roller if it is left unwashed overnight.

The problem often arises of how to paint the wall behind central heating radiators. It doesn't arise if you have a reflective foil behind them but it may be possible to ease the joint connections slightly so that a radiator brush can be used. Where many pipes have to be painted, especially central heating runs, a pipe brush will give a better coverage than the normal flat one.

Painting Doors and Windows

Dust is the biggest enemy of a good quality finish to paint on doors and windows, so it is essential to vacuum or sweep all floors and surfaces and try to maintain a dust-free working area. Try also to keep the paint in the can free from dust by using a little at a time in a paint kettle and by keeping the paint tin closed. And if you have any doubts about dust in the paint, filter it through an old nylon stocking.

There is a recognized sequence of painting doors and window frames (especially sash windows) which should be followed to give the best results. The illustrations show clearly the order in which they should be done.

As it is almost certain that gloss paint will be used for this work it will be worth it if you can obtain what the craftsman calls a 'mirror finish', in other words, a smooth glass-like finish with a depth of paint which will last for years.

This entails adequate preparation of the woodwork, filling in any tiny cracks with a stopping compound and sanding off any surplus. A suitable undercoat is then firmly brushed on in a criss-cross action and allowed to dry thoroughly. This is then lightly rubbed down with a waterproof glasspaper dipped in water.

When you are satisfied that the surface is smooth to the touch, apply

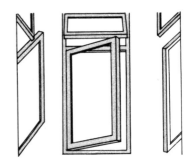

Shaded area denotes outside colour

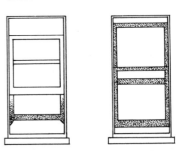

Panelled doors should be painted in the order shown

(*Left*) Top sash down   Bottom sash up
(*Right*) Position of windows when painting is completed

another undercoat so that you have built up a considerable thickness of paint. This is again rubbed down gently with the fine glasspaper and dried preferably with a chamois leather ; never use a fluffy duster.

Depending upon the effect you want to achieve you can now gently apply your finishing gloss coat, feathering off the surface with light upward strokes.

Always use a matching undercoat. Beginners often find it difficult to ensure that no places are overlooked when using Brilliant White gloss paint over a white undercoat. You can overcome this problem by working to the sequence illustrated or by arranging additional lighting at an angle to the work.

Brush Care

Many amateur decorators make their work more difficult and more costly by neglecting to care for their equipment. This is particularly so with brushes and rollers. A craftsman will tell you that it takes time for a new high-quality brush to get 'worn in', but it will be superior to a new one when it reaches this stage, so it is really a waste to neglect a brush merely because it is so easy to get another one.

Every home decorator should keep a small stock of brush cleaners, turpentine and patent cleaners. Some are general purpose cleaners, but some are solely for oil-based paints. Look at the label on the bottle. Dulux Brush Cleaner and Renovator, for example, can be used for storing brushes in between jobs because it evaporates slowly. Polyclens Plus, on the other hand, removes oil-based and similar

paints from brushes and rollers, but is not intended for emulsion or cellulose paints and must not come into contact with plastics, including thermoplastic floor tiles.

If at all possible brushes and rollers should be cleaned immediately after use. Excess paint should be squeezed out of the bristles or roller with a piece of wood, rinsed in the correct cleaner and finally washed in water and detergent. They should be allowed to dry before storage. A rubber band placed over the bristles will keep the brush in shape. You can assist the drying process by rolling the handle between the palms of the hands in a fast motion which will throw off excess moisture. Finally, wrap the brushes and roller in polythene and store in a warm, dry place.

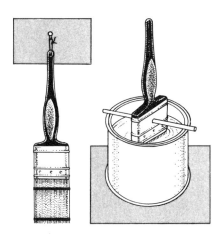

(*Left*) Wet brushes should be hung up to dry before they are put away (*Right*) Between painting jobs, suspend brushes in water or brush softener

23

Wall-coverings

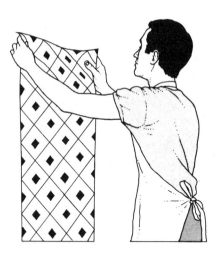

Wallpaper was the standard material for walls for many years until the new range of wall-paints and new types of wall-coverings came on the scene, but it wasn't until about thirty years ago that it became available to the home decorator. The standard variety was made from pulp and the few patterns available which were repeated year after year were known as 'porridge' papers because people continually asked for them.

As home decorating became more popular (and easier) great strides in the manufacture were made resulting in the tremendous variety of types of wall-coverings available today. But in spite of this progress wallpaper still provides the easiest (and possibly the cheapest) method of putting an attractive finish to a plain wall.

It will be helpful to consider the merits and types of wallpaper first. Simplest of all are the lining papers. These are available in various grades and have two main purposes. They are used to cover ceilings and walls that have imperfect surfaces or that have been already painted using oil-based paints and are then painted over, or used as a base for the heavier and more expensive wall-coverings, particularly the embossed types. If you propose to paint over these lining papers choose one of the special finished types. Standard wallpaper paste is used.

Next in the price range are the 'ingrains' or wood-chip papers and other 'duplex' (two layer) papers which have other materials sandwiched between. These are usually left white for painting and very attractive textured effects can be obtained. They are particularly useful on bad or unevenly plastered walls.

Great strides have been made in the designs and colourways of modern standard wallpaper and they represent excellent value for the money. The pattern and colour is printed directly on to the paper and then a thin coating is applied to fix the colour. Some care is needed to hang these papers, the lighter ones being hung immediately after pasting with a standard paste, while the heavier types should be left to soak up the paste for a few minutes. If you hang these papers in too much of a hurry they will shrink as they dry out showing gaps where the lengths should meet.

Next in the long line are what are called washable wallpapers. There has been a lot of argument as to what is 'washable' and it is recognized that the term 'spongeable' is more appropriate. These papers have a clear resin emulsion coating on the surface to protect the colour and pattern and are particularly suitable for bathrooms, kitchens and nursery rooms. Stains and grease can be sponged off with a mild detergent. As the surface is impervious to moisture a heavier paste containing a fungicide should be used. Some of these papers are strippable as the coating can be pulled off separately.

Still in the wallpaper range are the 'flock' types. To produce these the pattern is printed with an adhesive and while it is still active fine particles of fibres are blown on it to produce a pile effect. In a dusty atmosphere these flock papers are best cleaned with a vacuum cleaner.

Also in the paper field are the relief types. These are very thick papers for permanent fixture as once applied they are difficult to remove. They include such types as pebbledash and formal patterns and are intended for subsequent painting.

With vinyls we leave the wallpaper range, although the tough vinyl coating made from PVC (polyvinyl chloride) is welded to a stout backing paper. The colour printing is done with PVC inks. Vinyls which are also available in ready-pasted form are tough, moisture resistant and can really be scrubbed to remove grease and stains. For the non-pre-pasted type a heavy-duty paste is recommended to apply them to the wall. Removal is simplicity itself as the vinyl coating will come away easily from its backing, providing this has been securely fixed. New wall-coverings can then be applied directly on to the backing which becomes, in effect, a lining paper.

This description of wall-coverings would not be complete without a mention of the latest ICI product Novamura. As its 'new wall' title implies, it is an entirely new concept in decorating, as you paste the wall not the wall-covering. It is made from polyethylene film with a foam-like construction and if you wish to remove it, it strips off cleanly and easily in one piece, leaving no backing paper.

Many other materials, such as silk and velvet, have been used to cover walls but most of these are very difficult for the beginner to hang successfully. Hessian, however, is appealing and is supplied in standard lengths on a backing paper. There are coloured varieties, or natural (for subsequent painting), but care is needed to get the joins as close as possible otherwise the lines will always be obvious.

Wall veneer made from expanded polystyrene is a good form of insulation; it is particularly useful when applied to cold walls where condensation is a problem. A brittle substance, it is first applied dry to a pasted wall (use a heavy-duty paste made up to the instructions given) by rolling on and smoothing over. When firmly fixed, a paper or vinyl is hung overlapping the joins in the wall veneer. It is important to remember that walls treated in this way have a soft surface which is not resistant to knocks and damage by young children.

Tiles can also be used as a wall-covering, and methods of application are found on page 44.

Choosing Wallpaper

Wallpaper manufacturers normally produce a new set of wallpapers every two years, but if any of their designs are especially popular they may keep certain patterns running for much longer. Each batch printed has a number to indicate that the shading of the colours used is standard throughout the batch.

Bulk supplies go from the mill to the large wallpaper wholesalers who produce pattern books combining what they believe are the best available from several mills, or they may be collections from one specialist manufacturer. Often they are given their own numbers and this sometimes leads to confusion.

When you see 'room-lots' for sale (usually in packs of seven to eight rolls) it is likely that these are remainders from a bulk supply. They are sold at much lower prices and, if they are in good condition, of the same printing batch and the design is suitable, they represent a very good buy for the beginner. But you must be sure that there is sufficient to satisfy your requirements, for additional rolls may be very difficult to obtain.

For your first effort at paper-hanging it is not advisable to purchase a thin paper nor an expensive one. Choose a medium-weight one which is not pre-pasted, as you will want to get all the experience you can at paper-hanging before you undertake further redecoration and before you start using expensive materials. Give yourself a try-out in an unimportant room, perhaps the smaller of the bedrooms.

The secret of good paper-hanging can be summed up in one sentence : measure twice and cut once. To find out how many rolls may be needed walk round the room with a roll of paper and mark the walls with a pencil to find number of lengths of paper required, remembering to allow 50–75mm (2–3in) extra for cutting at the top and bottom.

With large patterned paper you should choose a part of the pattern to form the line along the ceiling or picture rail and measure the lengths from this point. If the distance is not more than 2.5m (8ft) you can expect to get four lengths from each roll. Depending upon the drop in the pattern (see examples) you will find you can avoid wastage by cutting lengths from alternate rolls. As you cut each length lightly number each one from 1 onwards in pencil.

Before cutting examine the paper carefully as some papers may be hung the wrong way up and you won't

Lengths can be matched by arranging them over a table.

(*Left*) Free match (*Right*) Drop repeat

notice this until it is too late. If the paper has a heavy floral pattern some shading will show beneath flowers and leaves and the right way up will be clearly indicated. But an intricate design of twining leaves should indicate that they twine upwards. The right way may be difficult to ascertain but you can usually take it that the free end of the roll goes to the top. If it doesn't look quite right rewind the roll and start again.

Matching patterns, especially intricate ones, are sometimes something of a puzzle. Papers are in four recognized types : plain (where no matching is necessary), free match (where there is a clear indication that any part will freely match another), set pattern (where the design repeats horizontally) and drop pattern (where the design repeats diagonally across the width).

Cutting lengths of a free pattern is quite simple as the first measured length will act for all subsequent ones. Set patterns are just as easy if you ensure that when you roll out successive lengths the pattern motif coincides exactly with the same motif in the previous length. Allow a little extra at the top in case the ceiling line or the picture rail is not perfectly horizontal.

Extra care is needed when dealing with drop patterns. When you have cut the first length make sure that the second piece comes exactly midway between two similar matching points in the first length, by matching its back edge with the front edge of the first piece. Allow a little extra top and bottom for trimming. See illustrations.

27

Removing Old Wallpaper

It is never advisable to apply a new wallpaper over an old one, the only exception being that in a very old property it might be difficult to remove a paper without bringing with it masses of plaster. In such a case the existing paper should be coated with emulsion paint before applying the new paper.

Removing old wallpaper can be a tiresome and messy job requiring plenty of patience and muscle power, but it is easier if you can assist penetration of the water by the addition of a branded wallpaper stripper. If not it is a question of repeated soaking to get the water through to release the paste.

If you suspect that the plaster under the paper is of a sandy nature it might be worth trying to remove the paper dry. Easing up the bottom with a stripping knife and gently pulling may give you hope that the whole piece will come off in one sheet.

However, as adequate preparation is vital to success the old paper should come off whenever possible. Use the largest possible brush, add a little detergent to the warm water and soak an area that is within easy reach. Do the upper parts first and work on about 2sq m (6½sq yd). With the stripping knife held at a fine angle, to prevent it from digging into the plaster, remove as much as you can in one upward sweep. The smaller pieces can be dealt with later. As you clear each area scrub it over with the brush or sponge to remove any scraps of paper and old paste. Change the water regularly.

If you have placed polythene or dust sheets on the floor you can leave the collection of strippings until you have done one wall, as the strippings will help to soak up excess water when you finally wash over the walls.

Removing painted wallpaper presents different problems. If an oil paint has been used and the paper appears to be securely fixed it is better not to try to remove it. Rub down any gloss until a smooth matt surface is obtained and then apply a lining paper fixed with a paste containing a fungicide.

If the paper has been painted with emulsion paint you have got to cut through the coating in order to permit the water to soften the paste. A wire brush can be used, while the patent scraper illustrated earlier is effective. A broken hacksaw blade fitted into a pad-handle can also be used.

It is sometimes very tempting to take an easy way out when redecorating a room. This applies particularly when a wallpaper has been properly fixed but you want to change its appearance. Some patterned wallpapers may require at least two coats of a good quality emulsion paint before the colours can be hidden and that means when you finally want to remove it the job will be more difficult.

Vinyl wallpapers are easy to remove as the adhesive holding the vinyl coating to its backing paper is different from the paste used to fix it to the wall. This means that you can part the vinyl at the bottom of the wall and by pulling on the corners remove the whole length, leaving behind the backing paper.

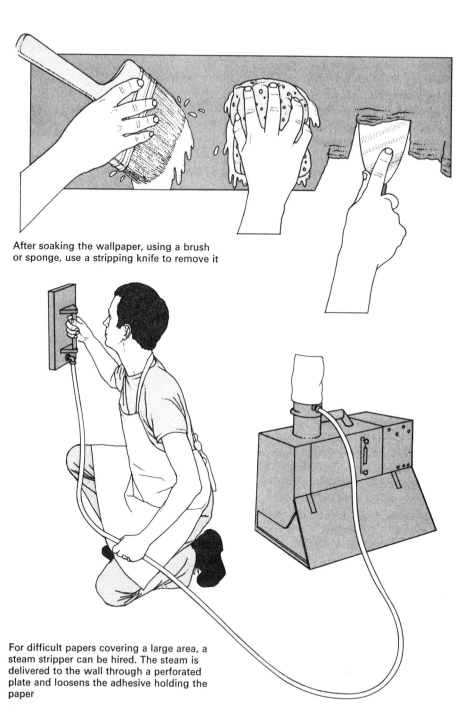

After soaking the wallpaper, using a brush or sponge, use a stripping knife to remove it

For difficult papers covering a large area, a steam stripper can be hired. The steam is delivered to the wall through a perforated plate and loosens the adhesive holding the paper

29

Hanging Wall-coverings

With the equipment illustrated (see p. 36) and a little patience, hanging a normal wallpaper is not a difficult task. Pasting tables are made with either a hardboard or plywood top, the former being slightly cheaper. If you get the plywood too wet there is a tendency for the top layers of ply to lift and splinters can result. If the hardboard gets too wet it may bulge or warp unless you dampen the rear surface when you put the table away to compensate for the moisture content. While the pasting table is the correct thing to use it is not absolutely vital, as a painted or varnished flush door placed upon suitable supports will suffice, especially if, later on, you decide to use only ready-pasted wall-coverings which makes pasting-brush, bucket, etc, superfluous. You will also need a measure—the modern type of metric straight edge is recommended.

If you are using lining paper, it is best applied immediately after it is pasted. It is hung horizontally allowing a slight overlap at each end which will be trimmed to the corners. Not all walls are perfectly flat or vertical. Part lengths are best cut and filled in as you proceed.

Pasting wallpaper is something of an acquired art, for it is most important that the paste is spread evenly (and without lumps) and that the edges are well covered. You can use either a ready-mixed paste or one made up strictly to the manufacturer's instructions.

If this is your very first effort at paperhanging you can make the job easier by 'sizing' the wall in order not only to seal a porous surface but to permit you to slide the paper into position, especially if you have a tricky pattern to deal with. Glue-size is no longer used for this purpose. A thinned mixture of the paste, made up to the proportions suggested on the packet, is quite suitable.

An experienced paper-hanger would place several lengths of paper on the table, paste one and fold it and paste another before hanging the first length. But I suggest that it will be easier if you follow the method described here.

First line up a length of paper with what will be the top against the right hand end of the table, with the back edge of the paper to the back edge of the table. Then paste the top quarter of the paper as shown in the sketch. If you always keep the edge of the paper you are pasting against the edge of the table, the paste brush need never come into contact with it, and this should ensure that the front surface of the paper is kept free from paste—but always keep a sponge and clean water handy to clean any paste that does get on the table.

You can check that the paste is of the right consistency and has been applied correctly by placing the brush on the corner which has been pasted. If you find the paper will lift off the table with the brush then all is well. If it doesn't then your paste is too weak or you haven't put enough on.

Now paste the second quarter overlapping the first slightly. When you've done this move the paper to the front edge of the table and paste the other two quarters.

To paste the rest of the length you will need to make a fold, and this should be about 40–45cm (15–20in). If the length you are pasting is a full 2.5m (8ft) or so you may have to make several folds in a concertina fashion.

Finish off the pasting by doing the back edge and the front. Beginners will find this a surer method of pasting than simply whacking on the paste in the centre of the paper and brushing out to the edges.

If the room has a chimney breast, or other outstanding feature, and you are using a paper with a prominent pattern, you should hang the first length at the centre of this feature and then progress to the right. Otherwise it is customary to start at one side of the main window and progress to the door and then return to the other side of the window and once again finish at the door.

It will be necessary, of course, to hang your paper vertically. This means that the first length must be absolutely straight. Use a plumb-bob and line and

if you are starting in a corner hang the line about 10mm ($\frac{1}{2}$in) short of the paper width, so that you can cut into the corner which may not be a true right angle. If you hang the paper into such a corner the rest of the lengths, when butted together, will simply exaggerate the error.

A long length of pasted wallpaper will obviously have to be handled with care, and you will need some kind of apron with a pocket in which to keep a smoothing brush and scissors so that both hands are free to manoeuvre the paper. Hold the pasted paper over your arm, climb on to your step ladder, or other sound support, and let the paper unfold slowly. You can reduce the chance of tearing by steadying the paper with your foot.

Now position the paper to the vertical line keeping the other edge clear of the wall so that only a narrow strip makes contact with the wall. You are then able to shift the paper easily into place. Then brush down from middle to outer edges of the paper to press out any bubbles of air.

At the join of the wall and ceiling mark the line with the scissors, pull the paper away and cut off any surplus. Do the same with the bottom of the paper at the skirting board and wipe off any paste on the paintwork.

All subsequent lengths are butt-jointed although it is worthwhile remembering that when you use relief papers to be emulsion painted it is better to leave a small gap which the emulsion paint will fill.

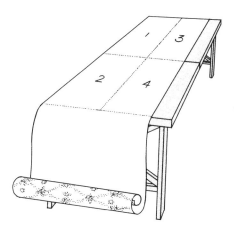

Ready-pasted Wall-coverings

Ready-pasted wallpapers are certainly a boon to amateur decorators because they reduce the need for equipment and are easy to apply.

With the paste already applied, the only equipment you need is a pair of steps, a sponge and seam roller, a pair of scissors and a trough to hold water. The paste is activated by immersing the paper in the water. You need a plumb-bob for marking the vertical lines and a straight-edge to measure up your cut length.

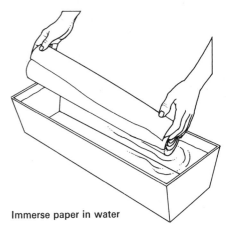

Immerse paper in water

Apart from these points, hanging ready-pasted papers is simplicity itself if you take care to see that the paper is immersed for the time recommended by the manufacturers (usually one minute), and that you don't kick the trough of water over the floor, or slop it about as you move it.

It is, of course, essential that high quality ready-pasted vinyl wallpapers should be hung upon sound walls. Cracks and holes should be filled and sanded smooth. Very porous walls should be given a coat of vinyl adhesive (which contains fungicide to prevent mould formation) diluted as directed. If you propose to hang these vinyls on oil-painted walls, you must reduce the gloss by sanding, and follow this by cross-lining with a good quality lining paper.

Having cut the lengths to the wall height, allowing a couple of inches for trimming top and bottom, loosely re-roll a length with the pattern inwards and immerse it in the water for the specified time. The trough should be two-thirds

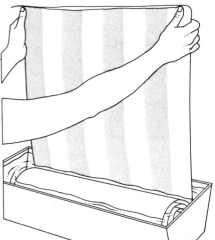

Lift slowly out of trough to allow excess water to drain off

full of cold water.

With the trough placed next to the wall, lift the paper slowly so that it unwinds in the water, wetting the back of the paper thoroughly and allowing the excess water to drain back into the trough.

Put the paper to the wall correctly positioned and smooth out any air bubbles from the centre to the edges

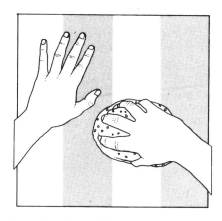

Smooth out air bubbles

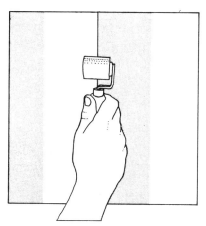

Fix edges with seam roller

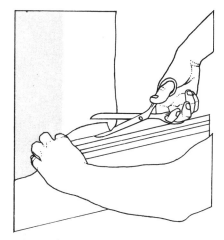

Trim surplus

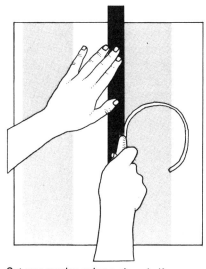

Cut any overlap using a sharp knife

with a damp sponge. Do this thoroughly, as once air bubbles are trapped they can't escape through the impervious vinyl coating. Trim top and bottom. To make sure the edges are firmly fixed run a seam roller lightly up and down. If the corners of the room are not perfect right angles, or where you find the lengths overlap slightly you will also find that vinyl will not stick to vinyl.

There are two ways of dealing with this. One is to lay a steel straightedge across the overlap and cut through with a sharp knife or razor blade. Remove the slight excess of paper and you will have a perfect butt joint. The second is to lift the overlap and apply a latex (rubber based) adhesive. Do this carefully as any excess will show.

33

Painting Ceilings

12-15in

Painting a plain plastered or plasterboard ceiling with oil-based paints is not a job for the inexperienced decorator. Not only must the paint be applied very evenly in wide strips with a full coat of paint and 'laid off' across them but it is difficult to avoid brush marks which become very noticeable under certain lighting conditions.

Full gloss paint, however, is only used in particular conditions or where special effects are required and you will probably find an emulsion paint to adequately suit your needs. These are now available in many types of finishes. There is a silk or semi-gloss type which should satisfy anyone who wishes to have a ceiling which will reflect more light.

Whichever paint is used for ceilings it is vital that you should be able to apply it without subjecting yourself to unnecessary physical strain. You should try to work on a strong scaffold board, firmly supported at both ends and at a height so that your head is about 30–40cm (12–15in) from the ceiling.

As the figure shows, the bent arm is comfortable and the eyes can see where the paint has been applied. For ceiling work a 100mm (4in) brush is normal but if you can handle a larger brush a larger area can be covered more quickly. But choose one which doesn't put too much strain on your wrist and arm. Try to cover an area of about 100 × 60cm (3 × 2ft) at a time joining up to a wet edge of the previous area. Don't drag a wet area to a dry one.

When you are using a brush with liquid emulsion paint you will undoubtedly find that the paint runs down the bristles on to the handle. To overcome this don't take up too much paint at one time. Dip the brush into the paint up to about one-third of its bristle length and gently tap it on to the sides of the can or paint kettle. Don't press it across the brim as this action removes most of the paint in the bristles, some of which will undoubtedly run down the outside of the can.

To stop any paint running down the handle wipe the brush occasionally across into the paint, and now and again brush down the inside of the can to stop any build-up of paint.

When using a roller for ceiling work you will need a paint tray. Use a 15cm (6in) or 18cm (7in) lambswool or mohair roller as these give a better finish than the sponge type which are likely to flick paint everywhere if they are pressed too hard against the surface. Don't overfill the paint tray which must stand on a firm surface—not on top of your step-ladder.

Dip the roller about half-way into the paint and then roll it up and down gently on the serrated shallower part so that the paint is well distributed on the roller. You can tackle large areas with a roller provided you can keep the last-painted edges wet. Don't try to roll out the paint too far or it will not cover properly. Move the roller from side to side and crosswise to get an even coverage.

The roller cannot reach into the corners of ceiling and wall and these parts should be painted using a 1 in brush. Do this just before you cover in with the roller otherwise there will be a difference in the texture between the finished effects.

Non-drip, or thixotropic, paints make a special appeal for ceiling work as, used direct from the can, a thick coating can be applied with very little brushwork needed to spread it evenly. However, as it liquefies with brushing it can also run down the handle unless you occasionally wipe the bristles over the rim of the can. You can use a roller with non-drip paints too, but the paint must be worked in the paint tray until it is sufficiently liquid to coat the roller evenly. If you take up lumps of paint on the roller they will spin off.

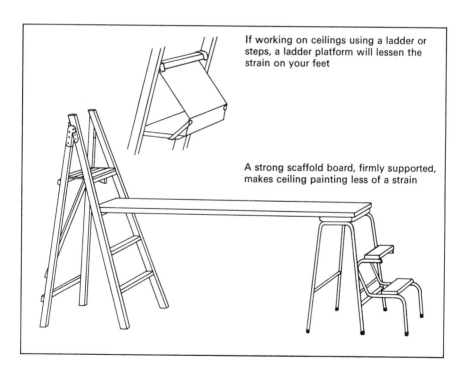

If working on ceilings using a ladder or steps, a ladder platform will lessen the strain on your feet

A strong scaffold board, firmly supported, makes ceiling painting less of a strain

Papering Ceilings

All kinds of ideas have been presented to encourage beginners to overcome their fear of failure when they consider that a ceiling needs papering : platforms to hold the pasted paper on spring-loaded poles, soft brooms, wires and all sorts of appliances beloved of the cartoonist. However, if the job is tackled in the correct way it becomes a matter of pride and self-satisfaction.

The paper must be adequately pasted, be folded in concertina fashion with pleats of about 40cm (15in) and you must be able to 'walk the plank' set at a convenient height so that you experience no strain on nerves or muscles.

Work always from the source of light, with the first length hung parallel to the window, although this may mean that longer lengths will be necessary. If it gives you more confidence, you can work with smaller lengths across the room.

Once you have positioned the first pleat and tapped it into the corner, move to your left pulling out the next fold. Brush along the edge and then across the width.

Most post-war houses have plasterboard ceilings with a coating of textured paint and these cannot be papered without the messy job of removing the paint, but plain ceilings can be covered with a textured or relief paper for subsequent painting.

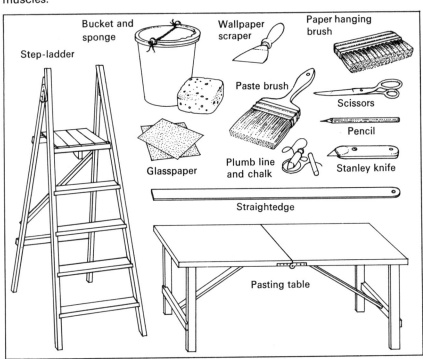

Bucket and sponge

Step-ladder

Wallpaper scraper

Paper hanging brush

Paste brush

Scissors

Pencil

Glasspaper

Plumb line and chalk

Stanley knife

Straightedge

Pasting table

Paper folded for ceiling, with roll for support

Begin at the lightest part of the room, using a roll of paper to support the cut length

3–9in

The best position when papering a ceiling

An adjustable tower platform makes ceiling decoration much easier

Other Ceiling Treatments

Most ceilings can be given an entirely new decorative treatment by one of the following methods : textured paints, Novamura film, fibrous plaster panels, embossed, carved and plain expanded polystyrene tiles, decorative tiles in rigid plastics, acoustic and insulating panels set in aluminium channelling and illuminated panels of plastics set in similar metalwork.

Of these the application of textured paint is the simplest and probably the cheapest. Polytex, for example, is a self-texturing material which is flexible enough to fill and keep covered cracks up to 2mm ($\frac{1}{16}$in) wide and is available in a range of six pastel shades as well as white. It is applied by brush or roller and can be given special textures by the use of pattern makers such as graining combs.

The standard white ceiling tile made from the very effective insulating material of expanded polystyrene is used in countless homes on kitchen and bathroom ceilings where it reduces condensation by keeping warm the surfaces to which it is applied. Unfortunately, it gets dirty when left in its natural state and, once fixed and the adhesive is dry, it should be coated with an emulsion paint. Oil paint must not be used. There is a fire-retardant emulsion paint available which can be used.

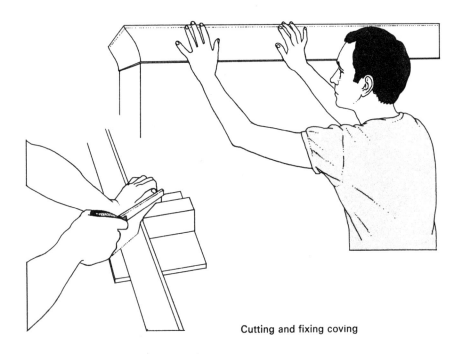

Cutting and fixing coving

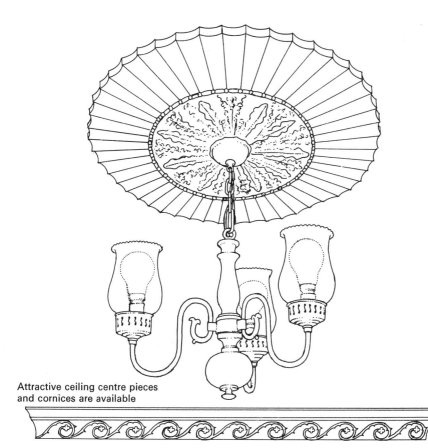

Attractive ceiling centre pieces
and cornices are available

Also to reduce any possible fire hazard the tiles should be coated overall with the correct adhesive and not put up by placing blobs of adhesive in the corners and centre. This method leaves an air space between tile and ceiling which fire officers believe increases the spread of flame.

Many attractive embossed and 'carved' expanded polystyrene tiles are now available and well worth considering as a useful form of ceiling decoration. One new development in this form of ceiling decoration is the VR Symphony series of extra thick tiles which make a continuous overall pattern, while there are four different designs to match traditional or modern room settings. There was a time when highly ornate plasterwork on ceilings was the hallmark of a palatial home but with the disappearance of the craftsman very little is to be seen. However, a new development in the technique of producing fibrous plaster means that very attractive ceiling centre pieces and attractive cornices can now be obtained.

Illuminated and Suspended Ceilings

One of the most interesting trends in modern interior decoration is the use of an illuminated ceiling, not only to give 'mood' lighting in the lounge or sitting room, but shadowless lighting in kitchens and bathrooms. There are the additional bonuses in the insulation it provides and the fact that further ceiling decoration is no longer necessary.

As the new suspended ceiling covers the old, however cracked and wavy it may be, there is no need for much extra work except to give it a coat of white emulsion paint to provide extra reflection.

A suspended illuminated ceiling is particularly useful in rooms with high ceilings, making quite a saving in their heating requirement. However, where the ceiling is already lower than the normal 2.45m (8ft) certain requirements must be taken into account.

Fitted normally, an illuminated ceiling requires a minimum of 90mm ($3\frac{1}{2}$in), to take the panels and the fluorescent gear, but if the ceiling is already low the lighting can be recessed into the present ceiling or accommodated in dropped box sections. In this case only 50–60mm ($2–2\frac{1}{2}$in) of ceiling height would be lost.

Of course, if an illuminated ceiling is not required acoustic panels can be fitted, or insulation panels used instead, to cut down transmitted noise to the room above. Alternatively, easy-to-clean light-reflecting panels can be substituted.

Panels are usually 60cm (24in) square in a wide variety of textured designs and conform to the fire safety of British standards and to the present building regulations. They are very light and simply rest in an aluminium framework.

The aluminium wall-angles are fixed around the walls, the main tees are then cut with a fine hacksaw and rested on the wall angles at about 60cm (2ft) intervals to form a grid pattern. The cross tees are then placed across at a similar distance. Remember that if the main tees are more than 3m (10ft) long they must be supported in the middle by a wire fixed to the ceiling.

Various lighting effects can be achieved by the use of dimmer switches. Details are supplied by the companies specializing in illuminated ceilings.

(*Opposite*) To fit an aluminium framework for a suspended ceiling: (1) Fit the perimeter angle trim around the walls at the required height using masonry nails (2) Fit the main runners and crosspieces to form a grid (3) Drop the panels into place

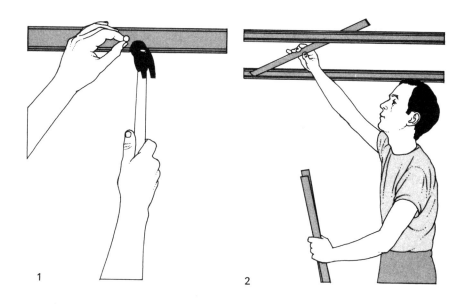

1

2

3

41

Floorings

No book on interior decorating would be complete unless it dealt adequately with the part that floorings play in the décor of the modern home. In making your choice of flooring you must take into account colour, texture and your existing or planned decorative schemes. The final selection from the bewildering number of types available will be determined, however, by the state of the sub-floor, which floor you wish to cover and the amount of money you have to spend.

As with every other form of home-improvement, preparation is all-important. Solid floors must be completely level. A self-smoothing screed, poured on and levelled roughly with a steel trowel, will fill up holes and depressions. A solid floor should show no signs of damp and before any attempt is made to cover it a test for dampness should be made. You can do this quite easily by taking a 50–75mm (2–3in) circle of plasticine and pressing a piece of dry glass on it so that air is excluded. After a day examine the underside of the glass and if you notice a faint haze then the solid floor—if recently laid—is still drying out, or if it is an old floor you may have a mild case of rising damp. The latter may be caused by a tear in the polythene damp course. Where damp is suspected, two coats of a waterproofing compound should be brushed on.

Timber floors should also be level. Examine the floor for loose boards, protruding nails or gaps. Nails should be punched down, and gaps filled with a wood filler and sanded level, but it is best to screw down loose boards as the nails holding them are probably loose. Unless you intend to leave the wooden floor exposed most timber floors will benefit by covering them with hardboard but before you do this make sure the underfloor ventilation is really efficient. The hardboard should be 'conditioned' before nailing down. The sheets must be scrubbed with a pint of water on the textured side and placed back to back for at least twenty-four hours. Hardboard is absorbent and if you put it down dry it will bend to the shape of the surface beneath should it become at all damp. The textured side should be uppermost when laying the board and hardboard nails must be used to fix it in place.

With preparation complete consideration can be given to the types of floor-covering available and their suitability to either timber or solid floors. Most coverings can be used on both floors but it is imperative that the surface is smooth and level. Vinyl tiles are used on both timber and solid floors although it is better to use vinyl asbestos tiles on the latter as they will tolerate slight damp. Cork tiles can be used on either floor—as can sheet vinyl, parquet, woodstrip, ceramic tiles. Quarry tiles are best used on solid floors only. Finally, carpet tiles and canvas- or foam-backed carpet may be used on both timber and solid floors.

It is sometimes difficult to choose between sheet vinyl and vinyl tiles. Both have distinct advantages. Sheet vinyl produces an all-over flooring with very few joins and seams and is available up to 3.66m (12ft) wide.

There is also a wider range of patterns, some with a cushioned effect. Its slight disadvantage is that in time it will shrink slightly so an overlap of 10mm ($\frac{1}{2}$in) should be left at a join until the final fixing a few weeks later. Tiles are much easier to fit but their position must be planned carefully otherwise a monotonous squared pattern can result.

Cork floor tiles give a luxurious feeling to floors. They are soft and quiet and when they are supplied with a coating of clear vinyl are very hard-wearing and easy to clean. Other types are unfinished and must be lightly smoothed and sealed. Waxed cork tiles are also available.

All forms of parquet wood flooring can be laid on timber or solid floors, using the special waterproof adhesive supplied. Parquet flooring blocks are a popular flooring with amateurs. They are 50–75mm (2–3in) wide × 23cm (9in) long and vary in thickness from 9.5–19mm ($\frac{3}{8}$–$\frac{3}{4}$in). Several

The appearance of wooden floors can be enhanced by using a sander from your local hire shop

interesting patterns can be made with them. Panels of parquet are about 25cm (10in) square and slot together over a cork underlay. There are also mosaic panels 9.5mm ($\frac{3}{8}$in) thick by about 45cm (18in) square which are fixed with a waterproof adhesive.

Strip flooring, usually 9.5mm ($\frac{3}{8}$in) thick and 44mm (1$\frac{3}{4}$in) to 70mm (2$\frac{3}{4}$in) wide is sold in lengths from 75cm (30in) to 3m (10ft) and can be applied to any level surface. Some are tongued and grooved to fit closely together or have lobes along each side to connect to matching strips. These are normally nailed in position, the nails being punched below the surface.

Ceramic tiles, available in a number of sizes, shapes and patterns with glazed or unglazed finish, will give you a lifetime of wear providing they are fixed correctly. Quarry tiles, made from red or brown clay, are usually unglazed and when fixed with special cements and bonding agents are sealed with a special oil-based liquid.

If you decide to use carpet, professional advice will be needed. Your local retailer will estimate and fit, most probably free of charge, the carpet you need. Canvas-backed carpet must be fitted by an expert—it has to be cut, bound and stretched properly. It will also need an underlay, usually corrugated rubber or sometimes felt. Foam-backed carpet is more easily dealt with by the amateur as it can be cut with scissors and does not need the stretching or binding of the canvas-backed. You will need a waterproof paper as an underlay. On tiled floors it is possible to use just newspaper.

43

Wall Treatments

While most of the wall areas in the home can be decorated quite satisfyingly with the normal wall-coverings there are certain areas where surfaces are required to stand up to more severe treatment. In kitchens and bathrooms there is the need for regular cleaning and the preservation of strict hygiene. Nothing is more suitable than ceramic tiling. Now that manufacturers have made the job so easy and attractive many millions of tiles are used every year, especially now the claim that they can be fixed to any sound surface has been proved justifiable.

Thorough surface preparation is important for successful tiling. The walls must be clean, flat, dry and firm. Any loose plaster should be removed and the wall filled ; a timber wall should be braced to prevent any movement or warping. For the home improver faced with the problem of removing cracked and crazed white tiles it is welcome news that he can tile over the old ones provided they are firm and thus save much time and a great deal of mess. One problem which often occurs with a fully tiled bathroom is bad condensation so make sure the room is adequately ventilated.

Ceramic glazed tiles are now sold in packs of fifty which will cover approximately 0.5sq m ($\frac{2}{3}$sq yd). Each tile, which has small spacer nibs or lugs, measures 108 × 108mm and is 4mm in thickness ($4\frac{1}{4} \times 4\frac{1}{4} \times \frac{5}{32}$in) A percentage of tiles in each pack are glazed on three sides for neat edges and external corners so you don't have

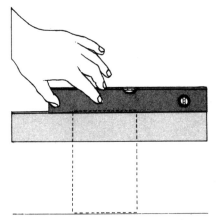

1 Mark the wall one tile height above the starting point and fix a lath

to worry about working out how many round-edged ones you might need.

The technique of tiling is quite simple. Fix lightly and perfectly horizontally a straight batten of wood one tile height at the bottom of the area you want to tile. Mark on the surface a true vertical line with a plumb-line or spirit level. This will give you a perfectly square starting point.

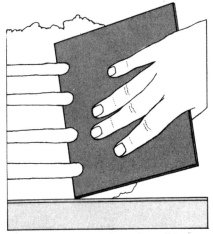

4 Use a grooved spreader to give a ribbed bed for the tiles

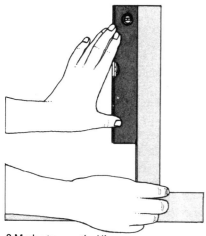

2 Mark a true vertical line

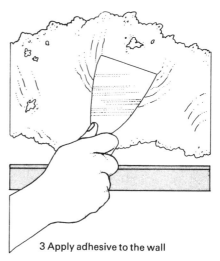

3 Apply adhesive to the wall

Spread the adhesive on the wall surface with a stripping knife over an area of about 1 sq m (1 sq yd). Then ridge the adhesive by drawing the grooved spreader over it. This will give you the ribbed surface necessary for good adhesion. Press the tiles in position, complete the bottom row and work up the wall. Some packs of tiles have self-spacing cards included in the pack which are placed between the tile edges but these are not necessary with spacer tiles.

After fixing wait at least twelve hours for the adhesive to set. Work a grouting compound into the joints with a sponge over an area of 1 sq m (1 sq yd). Remove any surplus with a damp cloth after it has started to dry out and polish the tiles with a soft cloth.

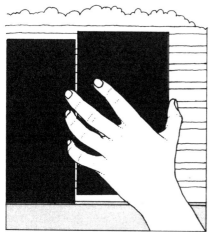

5 Press the tiles in position, starting from the left

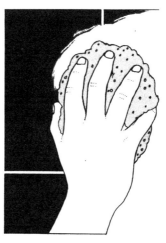

6 Work a grouting compound into the joints

Wall Treatments

Cutting tiles is not difficult providing you score through the glazed surface. Simply press each side of the tile over a matchstick underneath the score line and the tile will snap. Rough edges can be filed down if necessary using a carborundum stone.

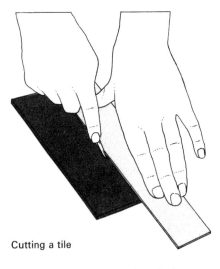

Cutting a tile

Border tiles are used for window ledges and reveals, half-wall tiling, external corners and splash-backs. These do not have spacer lugs so use small pieces of card to maintain even spacing.

If you are tiling over a half-tiled wall you have to decide how you will deal with the double thickness at the top. You can merely fill with grouting compound, use hardwood beading or put up a shelf. With each method you can continue above the half-tile wall if you wish.

Rigid plastic tiles are also available for bathrooms and kitchens. They are easily cut with a sharp knife and are fixed in position with glue. They require no grouting.

Attractive textured finishes can be obtained with thick coats of Polytex applied with a brush or roller. This covers up any imperfections of the wall surface and is very easy to apply. It is available in six colours: reef blue, birch grey, coral pink, pastel yellow, mint green and butter milk, plus white. Sold in plastic buckets, the spreading capacity of $2\frac{1}{2}$l is up to 6sq m (60sq ft).

Wall panels, wall boards and wall cladding lend themselves to a variety of uses by the enthusiastic home improver but covering a large area is likely to prove beyond his means. However, plain or patterned panels can be obtained in sixes of 2.74 × 1.25m (9 × 4ft) and 2.44 × 1.25m (8 × 4ft), while tongued and grooved planks 41cm (16in) wide and 2.44m (8ft) long with a knock-proof surface are available.

One way to introduce an interesting feature in a room is by way of using brick tiles. These are available in several shades, sizes and styles. Some are only 16mm ($\frac{5}{8}$in) thick and are merely stuck on a firm surface with the adhesive supplied. The quantity sold in each pack will cover $\frac{1}{2}$sq m (($\frac{1}{2}$sq yd). Brick tiles are normally used over fireplaces, on chimney breasts or feature walls.

With the growth of interest in brick decorative features an entirely new concept of wallcovering has arrived in the shape of WonderBrix, developed by Blue Hawk Ltd. It is a four-stage process. First a mortar base coat is spread over the wall and lightly stippled. Then the brick or stone pattern strips are applied. Thirdly, the texturing compound is trowelled on the wall over the strips. Finally, the strips are gently pulled away from the wall leaving what is a regular mortar course in the brickwork. The base coat will take 24 hours to dry and harden.

The cost works out at about £4 per sq m (sq yd). The base coat, that is, the joint colour, is available in white, black and grey. The texturing compound is in natural white, Portland buff, stock yellow and rustic red. The base coat is supplied in 1l buckets—enough to cover about 5sq m (50sq ft). The texturing compound comes in 10kg bags—enough to cover 3sq m (30sq ft). The tapes are bought in packs—each pack containing enough to cover 3sq m (30sq ft).

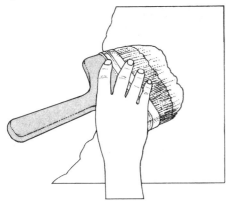

1 Spread mortar base coat over wall

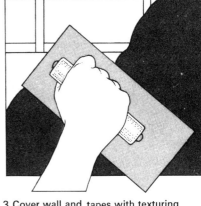

3 Cover wall and tapes with texturing compound

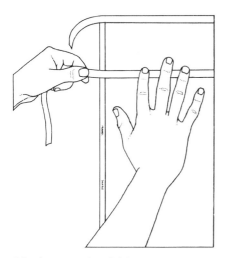

2 Apply tapes to form brick pattern

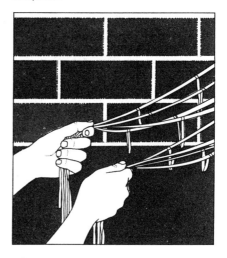

4 Remove tapes

Cornices, Covings and Niches

Nothing gives a more finished look to a room than an elegant cornice or coving. It smooths out and covers the unsightly angle between wall and ceiling which in new property often becomes an eyesore due to the shrinkage in the plastering. There are three different types to choose from : the standard gypsum plaster cove sold in 2m (6½ft) lengths about 100mm (4in) wide which is put up with the special adhesive supplied. It is easy to mitre for external and internal corners such as around the chimney breast or in alcoves as a template is provided. As it is fire resistant it has a special appeal for many people. Once installed it will last a lifetime. It will take about three hours to complete in a room

measuring 3.66 × 3.05m (12 × 10ft).

The second choice, although it will cost more, is to use an individually designed cornice in fibrous plaster or glass fibre. You can have a special design copied and reproduced in fibrous plaster by a firm specializing in the work.

Finally, there is a wide range of covings made from expanded polystyrene, very easy to put up with the recommended adhesive. Apart from the standard moulded cove, there are new profiles in the VR Vincel Symphony series range, for particular use with their matching tiles.

Another feature which gives any room a touch of elegance is a niche. Normally made of fibrous plaster they are cut into the wall as shown, but a corner fixing unit can also be obtained.

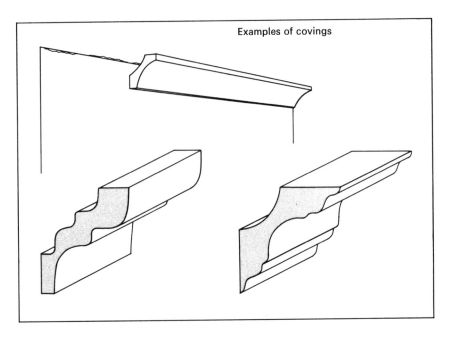

Examples of covings

Installing a niche

49

Plasterboards and Plastering

In most post-war houses certain sections of the first floor which do not have load-bearing walls are constructed of plasterboard partitioning.

Plasterboards are made of gypsum core sandwiched between two stout paper covers. They are available in eight lengths from 1.8–3.66m (6–12ft) and in widths of 60, 90 and 122cm (2, 3 or 4ft) and in two thicknesses: 10mm ($\frac{3}{8}$in) for use at 450mm (18in) centres and 13mm ($\frac{1}{2}$in) for more widely spaced 'studding'.

Studs are normally of 75mm (3in) × 50mm (2in) timber, although in recent years the soaring price of timber has meant that the builder may have used smaller material.

Plasterboards are fixed with special broad-headed galvanized nails at 150mm (6in) intervals, positioned no less than 13 to 15mm ($\frac{1}{2}$ to $\frac{5}{8}$in) in from the edges. Care must be taken in driving in the nails as it is easy to dent the plasterboard. The nail heads can be covered with filler. A slight gap about 13mm ($\frac{1}{2}$in) is left between the boards and is covered by a 90mm ($3\frac{3}{4}$in) wide jute scrim or special joint filler before a coat of plaster is applied over the whole wall.

It sometimes happens that in moving furniture large dents or even holes are made in the boards and these must be filled. One of the proprietary cellulose-based fillers would be quite suitable as these do not shrink so much as the normal plasters.

In houses built within the last few years there is always a fair amount of plaster shrinkage especially where plaster edges meet the woodwork, both of which shrink when the house dries out. Cracks in wall surfaces appear also where uneven shrinkage has taken place or where some movement from vibration or settlement has occurred.

It is not sufficient merely to fill these cracks with a cellulose filler. Open them up slightly to give a key to the new material. Use a putty knife to undercut the crack (see illustration), apply a little water with a brush and press in the filler, after making sure no dust has been left in the crack. Deep holes should be done in two stages, allowing the first part to harden before finishing off level.

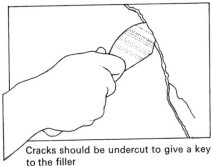

Cracks should be undercut to give a key to the filler

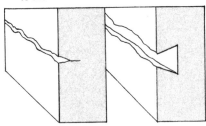

If you have much filling to do the job can be made easier by making yourself a small handboard out of a piece of plywood. You can mix small amounts of filler on the board or use one of the ready-mixed fillers.

Cracks between wall and ceiling have a nasty habit of resisting any attempt to fill them. You think you have done a very good job and are frustrated when the cracks appear a few weeks later. The cause is nearly always due to movement in the floor joists of the room above affecting the plasterboard ceiling. A stiff mixture of filler should be pressed hard into such cracks. If after a couple of attempts you cannot solve the problem, and the cracks become so obvious, you might consider fitting a coving or cornice as indicated on the previous pages.

Where plaster has broken away from solid walls, or where you have discovered damp patches which need replacement, a different technique is required using a patching plaster or 'Siraphite'. In such cases the plaster is applied in two coats : what is called a scratch coat and a finishing or 'setting' coat. The edges of the good plaster are cut in to give a key, the edges are damped and the plaster is applied with a trowel from the bottom of the area to the top, allowing about 3mm ($\frac{1}{8}$in) for the finishing coat.

When this first coat has almost set scratch lines are scored with the point of the trowel to assist the second coat to bind. The final coat of plaster is then applied and while it is setting a straight rule or piece of timber is laid across and moved upwards across the patch to level it off. When the area of new plastering is quite dry a little sanding may be necessary to give a matching smooth surface.

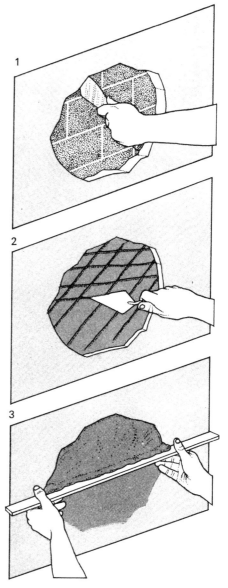

1 Cut back edges of existing plaster
2 Apply scratch lines to first coat of new plaster
3 Level off final coat of plaster

Lighting

Designers of modern houses seem to have little idea of what a modern family needs in the way of artificial lighting. They place one, or perhaps two, pendant fittings in the ceilings, and occasionally will arrange to provide points for wall lights. You also find that generally the number of socket outlets on a ring system is totally inadequate for family needs.

As a result uninformed persons plug in lamps to the ring circuit with incorrectly fused plugs with adapters and long trailing flexes which are a constant source of trouble. When they hide them under carpets they are simply asking for trouble. The most common mistake in home lighting is providing too much general lighting— particularly from overhead sources— and insufficient lighting in any one place to satisfy the requirements of particular tasks, such as for reading, sewing, etc.

Apart from these basic needs the function of lighting is to produce an effect to add interest to the home, to enhance furnishings and décor. Correct lighting can make all the difference to the shape and apparent size of a room. Directed to the floor it tends to lower the ceiling whilst the opposite effect is created by directing light to the ceiling. Similarly, by lighting the narrow walls of a room and softening the lighting of the wider walls a broadening effect is given to the room. Lighting an alcove gives the impression of extra room space. The placing of the TV set, which now competes with the fireplace as the focal point of a living-room, will control some of the lighting. Soft light should always be present to prevent eye-strain but it should not be reflected by the screen. A simple basic rule to remember is, light from above for general illumination, from the front for emphasis, from the side for modelling or shaping a particular piece of furniture and from below for special effect.

Consider also the new switch controls which can dim or change different circuits so that any mood can be created. Lighting in nursery rooms or in a small child's bedroom is most satisfactorily controlled with a dimmer switch.

The rating of the lamp bulbs is important. One cannot accept a single pendant fitting with a 100-watt bulb as being adequate for an average room. Upgrade it to 150 if the shade on the fitting will allow it without scorching. Table lamps should not be less than 100 watts and floor standards 150. A large room needs feature lighting :

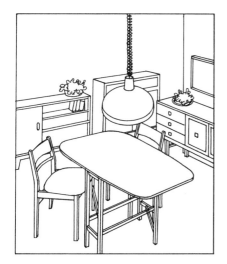 

Lighting arrangements should be designed to suit specific requirements in each room

fluorescent lights concealed by a pelmet above curtains, a spot-light on a treasured picture. Wall brackets can make a great difference to such a room.

The present trend in dining-room lighting (ignoring the soft intimate lighting of candles in attractive candelabra) is for a centre pendant with a rise and fall action directed over the centre of the dining table. The type of shade fitting is important, so choose one with almost opaque sides so that light is directed to the table and not into the eyes of the diners.

Bedroom lighting is usually designed for functional purposes—so that one can read in bed or see oneself in the dressing-table mirror. A single pendant light in the centre of the room is more or less useless for these requirements. Soft lights in bedside table-lamps which give a good reading light and are accessible for switching on and off are ideal. Lighting should not be above the mirrors on the dressing-table as it will cast reflections. It is better to illuminate the person rather than the mirror.

The ideal lighting for kitchens is the fluorescent strip light as there are many shiny surfaces which can create glare if filament lighting is used. Normally two strips are required with one essentially placed above and parallel with the edge of the sink.

Curtains and Fixings

Curtains can make or mar any room. It is no longer fashionable merely to look upon them as a means of shutting out light and giving a measure of privacy. They are an essential part of a room's décor, blending with the other decorative features and, in many cases, contributing considerably to the retention of warmth. Of course some attention should always be given to ensure that the windows are draughtproof.

There are a few points to remember when choosing or making curtains. Full length means 13mm ($\frac{1}{2}$in) from the floor; sill length is 100–150mm (4–6in) below the sill and recessed window length just brushes the sill.

In modern houses where most large windows have central heating radiators underneath it is important that the curtains should not overlap the radiators, but finish 50–75mm (2–3in) above them. Where condensation is a problem fabric curtains should always be at least 150mm (6in) from the glass, so this point should be borne in mind when fixing the track which should extend 150mm (6in) beyond the window on each side.

You can estimate the amount of material required by measuring the length of the track and if you decide upon ordinary gathers you will need 1$\frac{1}{2}$ times this width. Pencil pleats on Regis tape take from 2 to 2$\frac{1}{2}$ times this width. With a patterned fabric where the design must always be perfectly horizontal there will be some wastage, but this can be reduced to a minimum by measuring the length of the drop in

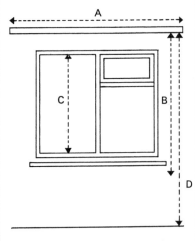

A Curtain track should extend 150mm (6in) either side of window
B Measurement for sill-length curtains
C Measurement for recessed window length
D Measurement for full-length curtains

the pattern (as you would do for wallpaper) and adjusting the length accordingly.

Wherever possible curtains should be lined. The linings will protect the face material from fading, give the curtains a better hang, particularly with thin cottons, and when drawn help to reduce exterior noise. The task of lining is made much simpler by the use of Rufflette detachable lining tape, which is hung on the same hooks used to hang the curtains. Loose linings have the great advantage of avoiding the effects of different shrinkage between curtains and linings woven in different materials.

There is a wide variety of curtain tracks in the shops and you will have to decide if you want to use one which requires a pelmet or valance or whether the rail will be exposed when the curtains are drawn back. Most rails are flexible enough to go round curves and most fittings allow curtains to overlap. Other rails, particularly Swish De Luxe, can be fitted with finials in gilt or white which add an attractive finish. Cording sets are available for most tracks.

Back into fashion for straight runs only are cornice poles in metal or wood. The curtains are hung on large rings which slide over the poles, or can be hung on rings attached to runners built into the rail. Some metal cornice poles are extendible making cutting to size unnecessary.

Fixing the track is not difficult when it has to be merely screwed into a batten over the window, but often it means that it must be fitted into a concrete lintel. Here you have a choice of using either a masonry drill to fix a batten with screws and plugs or fitting a cornice pole to overlap each end of the lintel. A batten fixed with masonry nails at 150mm (6in) intervals (use a nail 20mm ($\frac{3}{4}$in) larger than the depth of the batten and tap in carefully) will hold the heaviest of curtains.

Net curtains are usually hung on plastic-coated curtain wire, available in a roll for cutting to size. Use a round head screw each side of the frame and fit the screw eyes to the wire.

Roller-blinds, bought to size or made up from kits, are especially suitable in kitchens, cloakrooms and bathrooms. The instructions supplied with the kits are clear and self-explanatory and within the skill of any practical homemaker. These blinds are normally fitted into the reveals of a window.

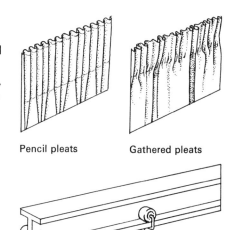

Pencil pleats   Gathered pleats

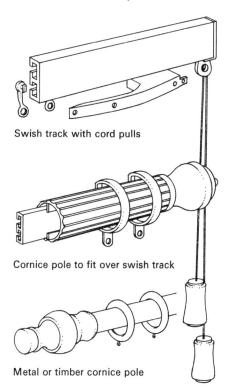

Brass track for use with pelmet

Swish track with cord pulls

Cornice pole to fit over swish track

Metal or timber cornice pole

Fixing Devices

There are many occasions when every amateur decorator needs to fix things. It may be a simple shelf, wall brackets, self-assembly units to walls which will be of different construction. They may be made of solid concrete blocks, aerated concrete, hollow breeze blocks or plaster partitioning and each will require separate techniques to ensure that whatever is fixed will stay in place and carry more than the weight to be placed on it.

The first question to ask yourself is whether it is safe to make a hole where you want it. There may be cables or pipes quite near the surface which can spell danger if they are pierced. It is never wise to take a chance, for if you meet with an obstruction you've only got to start somewhere else.

If you have a lot of fixing to do and are unaware of the cable and pipe runs in your property it will pay you to invest in one of the now popular metal detectors. For the present price of just under £6 you can get a D800 metal detector, powered by a PP3 battery which will detect hidden nails and water pipes and electric cables up to 10cm (4in) deep in floors or walls, thus removing any hazard.

While many lightweight items may be fixed with modern adhesives (see the following pages) basic items required are boring tools, screws and screwdrivers, or masonry nails and hammer. The electric drill with masonry bits will deal speedily with most wall surfaces, but one with a hammer effect will reduce effort when drilling into concrete. The Rawltool with a triangular pointed head will make holes in the hardest material but requires a certain amount of patience and muscle power.

If you use masonry nails on solid

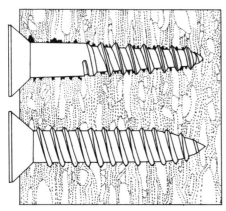

(*Above*) A typical wood screw
(*Below*) A Twinfast screw for use with chipboard

(*Opposite*)
1 A spring toggle can be attached to the screw which opens out to give a secure grip
2 Expanding plastic plug
3 Fibre plug
4 Plastic plug
5 Screw plug
6 Chipboard plug

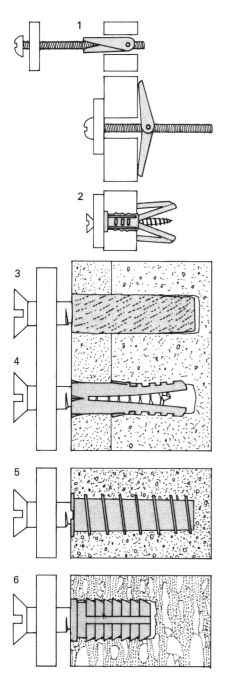

walls choose those of the right length. The packs will give details of how much nail should enter the wall, depending upon the thickness of the material you are fixing. Don't exceed this length.

When making holes in soft plaster or aggregate materials the hole often becomes much larger than required. In this case it is better to use a filler compound based upon asbestos wool and cement. This is wetted with clean water and made into a tight plug which is pressed into the hole. If this is for a fitting which may be changed later put a little grease on the screw before inserting it or the screw will corrode and be difficult to remove.

When fixing to plasterboard, fibre board or lath and plaster this will be normally fixed to timber studding at intervals of about 380mm (15in). If you can find these timber studs it may be possible to fix into them, giving a much more secure hold.

Where the framing cannot be used there is a limit to the weight the plasterboard can bear and expanding bolts or plugs must be used. These may be of metal, plastic or rubber (see illustrations).

For most normal fixing jobs Nos 8, 10 and 12 gauge screws are used and their sizes are 25mm (1in), 31mm (1¼in), 51mm (2in) and 64mm (2½in) in length. Always use a screwdriver to fit exactly the slot in the head.

Many items which have to be fixed with nails into hardwoods, plywood, hardboard and composition board, plastic faced materials can be attached with a heavy duty staple gun. The Arrow 1–50 gun will take six sizes from 6mm to 13mm (¼in to ½in).

Adhesives

There are many occasions when a glue or adhesive is required to join together similar or different materials in a permanent bond. There are so many different types available, including several for which claims are made that they will stick anything and everything.

As cost is an important factor in home maintenance there is little point, for example, in buying an epoxy resin adhesive which will certainly stick almost anything, when a cheaper type will adequately cope with one particular requirement. What has complicated the choice of glues is the vast range of new adhesives which technology has provided, from one-spot adhesives to new forms of panel adhesives applied by a gun.

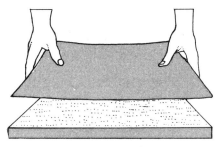

While even the top expert cannot explain *exactly* why and how an adhesive functions (some say molecular attraction, others say that exclusion of air between two almost perfectly flat surfaces brings atmospheric pressure into play) there are certain basic rules which should be followed when using every type of adhesive.

All surfaces to be joined should be dry (there are one or two exceptions), perfectly clean and free from dust and grease. Some surfaces should be as smooth as you can make them, others roughened up slightly so that the gap-filling glue can take a stronger hold.

There are several glues which have volatile solvents and give off a highly flammable vapour when used in quantity and it is absolutely vital not to smoke and to ensure maximum ventilation while using them. In the kitchen it is essential to see that any pilot light on cooker or boiler is turned off. If you have any doubt on this matter it would be better to use one of the emulsion-based adhesives marketed for similar use.

A favourite job of home-improvers is the fixing of the highly decorative plastic laminate sheets to work surfaces, built-in furniture, etc. This is a simple enough job and, with care, a professional finish can be achieved.

If you propose to cover a kitchen unit, for example, the plastic laminate should be cut with a fine toothed handsaw, or with one of the new laminate cutters to the exact size of the unit top. Strips should be cut to cover the edges.

For the adhesive you have the choice between at least two well known brands. Thixofix is a non-drip contact adhesive which is applied to the two surfaces, allowed to become tacky and then placed into position. The claim made for it is that if you get the positioning slightly wrong there is time to adjust it before pressing into position.

The other product is the new Non-Flam contact adhesive from Evo-Stik. This is an emulsion-based type which is of milky colour when it is applied, but changes to clear when it is ready for bonding thus removing the need to watch it carefully. This adhesive has the advantage that it will wash off your hands and brushes in water. Anyone who has used the older types will know what this advantage means.

The strips should then be applied to the edges and lightly hammered over a piece of softwood to assist adhesion. All edges can be gently planed or filed to smooth the edges and expose the undersurface of the laminate. You can do this very easily with a plastic laminate edging tool, which isn't very expensive.

Some Modern Adhesives—Types and Uses

Polythene must be heat welded.

Polyvinyl Acetate (PVA) for wood, paper, fabrics, card, leather
Brand Names: Bostik Stik 'n Fix ; Britfix Wood Glue ; Croid Polystik ; Dunlop Woodworker ; Evo-Stik Woodworker ; ICI Dufix ; Polybond ; Unibond

Epoxy Resins for metals, glass, rigid plastics, pottery, stone, wood, fabrics, leather

Brand Names: Araldite and Araldite Rapid ; Devcon 5 Minute ; Evo-Stik Hard and Fast ; Plastic Padding Super Epoxy

Contact Adhesives for wood, rigid PVC and plastic laminates, fabrics, rubber, leather
Brand Names: Bostik Contact ; Dunlop Thixofix ; Evo-Stik Non-Flam ; Rawlplug Durofast

Rubber-based Adhesives for rubber, leather, fabrics, wood, paper, metals, carpets
Brand Names: Copydex DIY Adhesive ; Devcon Rubber ; Jiffybind (by Copydex)

Polystyrene Cement for polystyrene plastics (not expanded or foam rubber)
Brand Names: Britfix Polystyrene ; Revell Polystyrene

Polyvinyl Chloride for PVC plastics, vinyls, leather, rubber, fabrics
Brand Names: Britfix PVC Adhesive ; PAC (by Copydex)

General Purpose for paper and card, wood, leather, canvas, fabrics, PVC and rigid plastics, glass and metal, plaster
Brand Names: Bostik Clear Adhesive ; Britfix Clear Adhesive ; Croid No 1 Tubes ; Evo-Stik Clear Adhesive ; Gloy Household Glue ; Rawlplug Durafix ; Unibond

Cyanoacrylate for metals, glass, most plastics, rubber, hardwoods
Brand Names: Cyanolit Instant Adhesive ; Loctite Super Glue-3 ; Permabond

Treating Damp and Condensation

Dampness and excessive condensation are the great enemies of interior decoration and though allied should be considered separately.

Normally, damp patches in the home are caused by penetration from outside ; through an ineffective damp-proof course (DPC) through porous brickwork ; by rain entering the chimney causing stains on the chimney breast ; or by careless brickwork whereby mortar has covered the metal wall-tie in the cavity making a bridge for dampness to pass to the inside wall. The effect of the latter is often seen in lifting wallpaper or bulging plaster, causing it to come away from the wall.

The effect of damp rising from a faulty DPC can be seen in discolouration and even wet rot of skirting boards on the ground floor. It is never wise to pile up soil above the damp-course ; always check that the airbricks to suspended floors are not blocked, and that gutters and downpipes are clear and do not overflow or leak when there is heavy rain. Lichen and mosses should not be allowed to accumulate on roofs as this prevents the tiles from drying out quickly.

Flat roofs, even those well constructed, are notorious for creating damp ceilings and should be regularly checked to see if the coverings are sound.

Defective damp-proof courses require special treatment outside the scope of this book, but something can be done to correct damp which enters from outside walls and around window frames.

Among the readily available products which have been well tested are :

Aquaprufe, a damp-proof membrane
Aquaseal 10, a floor surface waterproofer
Aquaseal 77, an interior damp proofing for walls and ceilings
Aquaseal 66, a water repellent for external walls
Synthaprufe, a brush-applied liquid which forms an elastic film over walls and floors
Synthasil, a silicone water-repellent for outside walls.
Granger's Proofing 1210, for brushing or spraying on damp or dry walls, inside and out, which does not seal

the surface but allows dampness to evaporate
Sealocrete Epoxy Wetcote, a two part mixture to damp-proof internal floors and brickwork, especially suitable for basement rooms
Q19, an epoxy emulsion paint for waterproofing internal surfaces.

Apply two coats of sealer to porous exterior brickwork

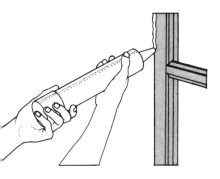

'dewpoint' is reached and the moisture is deposited.

Double-glazing counteracts this effect because the internal pane of glass is at almost the same temperature as that of the room—being insulated from the outside temperature by the air seal between the glass. But although double-glazing greatly reduces heat loss from the room, condensation may appear on walls adjacent to the windows, particularly when the wall is a large north-facing one.

In a single-glazed window, the glass which transmits heat very efficiently, is at a temperature equal to that outside, hence the heavy deposits of moisture, particularly when there is a big difference between internal and external temperatures.

It must be remembered that human beings exhale a vast amount of moist air throughout each day and in a room which is almost draughtproof and unventilated condensation must be accepted as a fact of modern life.

The following measures will help reduce condensation in the home:

1 Increase the amount of ventilation and ensure adequate insulation in each room.
2 Create warmer surfaces with a wall veneer underneath the wall covering.
3 Place carpets over tiled or solid floors.
4 Fit an extractor fan as high as possible in the kitchen to reduce the amount of moist air reaching other parts of the home.
5 In severe cases of condensation decorate with an anti-condensation paint.

Improving the Fireplace

With the open hearth becoming, once again, the focal point of the sitting-room/lounge there are many possibilities for its development as a feature by the enthusiastic home-improver.

The success which has attended the publicity campaign to 'open up your fireplace', the advice to local authorities to reintroduce fireplaces to their council house building programme, the introduction of highly decorative wood-burning stoves to use up the surplus of elm-logs have all contributed to this growing interest.

Suppliers of fireplace building materials, many providing designs and the kits to make them up, have contributed to make it possible for any handyman to equal the workmanship of a craftsman. Even the old-fashioned tiled fireplace with its wooden surround and mantelpiece can be given a facelift with reinforced glass-fibre mouldings and plastic 'carvings'.

Removal of the usual tiled surround is not a difficult problem as it is normally held in place by long screws through the frame into battens fixed to the wall. Where it has been cemented in place a few well-placed taps with a bolster chisel will cause it to part company with the wall.

Bibliography

Alexander, J. *Home Decoration* (Pelham Books, 1970)
Bowyer, J. *Central Heating* (David & Charles, 1977)
Day, Roy. *All About House Repair and Maintenance* (Hamlyn, 1976)
——, ——. *All About Plumbing and Central Heating* (Hamlyn, 1976)
Hall, E. and Wilkins, Tony. *Home Plumbing* (Newnes-Butterworth, 1977)
Johnson, David. *Home Improvements: A DIY Guide* (Stanley Paul, 1973)
McLaughlin, T. *Make Your Own Electricity* (David & Charles, 1977)
Reader's Digest. *Home Decorating* (Reader's Digest, 1976)
Richardson, S. A. *Protecting Buildings* (David & Charles, 1977)
Taylor, Alan. *Home Maintenance and Repairs* (MacGibbon and Kee, 1972)
——, ——. *Do-it-yourself Home Improvements* (Hart-Davis, 1975)
Do It Yourself, Link House, Dingwall Avenue, Croydon, Surrey CR9 2TA

Illustrated by David Ashby

British Library Cataloguing in Publication Data

Johnson, David, b.1906
 Home decorating. – (Penny Pincher; 11).
 1. Interior decoration – Amateurs' manuals
 I. Title II. Series
 643'.7   TH8026

ISBN 0–7153–7751–5

Set in Univers
and printed in Great Britain
by Redwood Burn Limited
for David & Charles (Publishers) Limited
Brunel House Newton Abbot Devon

Published in the United States of America
by David & Charles Inc
North Pomfret Vermont 05053 USA